#1 Reward
the Fox

#3 King of
Frogs

#8 Jabuti
last story

Forestville Tales

Aaron Berman

ALTA BOOK CENTER, PUBLISHERS
San Francisco, California USA

Library of Congress Catalog
Card Number: 76-56544

Illustrated by Harry Rosenbaum
Designed by Frank B. Marshall III

Alta Book Center Publishers–San Francisco
14 Adrian Court
Burlingame, California 94010 USA
Phone: 800 ALTA/ESL • 650.692.1285
Fax: 800 ALTA/FAX • 650.692.4654
Email: info@altaesl.com • Website: www.altaesl.com

Printed in the United States of America

Contents

For my daughter, Raquel

Introduction

To the Teacher:

Forestville Tales is a supplementary reader for young and young-at-heart learners of English as a foreign or second language. It contains eight short folk stories in simplified English. The folk stories represent many cultures, yet they touch on a commonality within the reader's experience and imagination. The ideas in each story cover the range from the sublime to the ridiculous, making the folk tales a refreshing change of pace from the standard language lesson.

Forestville Tales is designed to develop reading and speaking skills. The unique feature of *Forestville Tales* is that each story is sequentially illustrated. The illustrations give students a better understanding of the folk tales and can be used as cues when asking students to retell the stories in their own words. Segments of each story are numbered to indicate the corresponding picture on the opposite page.

Each lesson opens with a list of words and expressions, followed by the illustrated folk tale. There are a variety of short exercises that develop and reinforce reading and speaking skills. Whenever an exercise is presented for the first time, the student is given a model to follow. You should not feel compelled to go through all the exercises in each lesson. You may even wish to assign exercises individually, letting each student progress at his or her own rate.

Some Suggestions for Using *Forestville Tales:*

1. Before reading each story, explain the basic idea in a few short sentences.

2. Follow this brief introduction by explaining the words and expressions from the list which may not be familiar to your students.

3. Ask the students to open their books and read silently, as you read the story aloud. In this way, you maintain command of the pace and usually avoid classroom boredom caused by the slow, insecure reading of the students themselves.

4. After reading the story, you may want to ask the group which words or concepts they did not understand. Remember that the illustrations can be used to clarify difficult words or structures. Then re-read the story.

5. Ask your students sequential questions about the story, questions that can be answered by simply re-reading the folk tale. This type of questioning trains your students in the valuable skill of skimming and provides them with the opportunity to re-read effortlessly.

Phrase the questions so that they can be answered in both long and short responses that can be taken directly from the story (without asking the student to generate new language). Here is an example, taken from the first story:

It's winter. Renard the fox is very hungry, but he is not worried. He is a very smart fox. He knows that he can find food for his family without a lot of work.

Suggested sequential questions and possible answers:

a. What time of year is it? Is it summer or winter?
   Short response: Winter
   Long response: It's winter.

b. Is Renard hungry?
   Short response: Yes.
   Long response: Yes, he's hungry.

c. Is he a stupid or smart fox?
   Short response: Smart.
   Long response: He's a smart fox.

d. What does he know?
   Short response: (That) he can find food for his family.
   Long response: He knows that he can find food for his family.

Continue in the same vein, always following the sequence of the story when questioning.

6. Assign some of the exercises for class or individual seat-work. You may want to give out some of the exercises for homework.

7. Ask some of the sequential questions again, this time with books closed.

8. Tell students to cover up the written portions and retell the story by looking at the pictures. You may want to choose one student per picture, or one student for all of the pictures, or both.

Additional Activities:

1. Choose key phrases from the story and write a dialogue with the students. Have the students memorize the dialogue and dramatize the story in groups.

2. List connecting words (*so, then, and, but,* etc.), on the blackboard. Go over the words with the class, giving several examples of the impact these words have when used to connect two or more sentences into one. Then, choose a folk tale and show how a connecting word can be used to link the events in one illustration with the events depicted in the illustration immediately following.

3. Select an illustration from the story and ask students to describe what they see in the picture.

These short, adapted folk stories were developed during my years of teaching English as a second language to Cuban children at Everglades and Citrus Grove Elementary Schools in Miami, Florida, and teacher training at Sonoma State University in California. Several people are responsible for adding new dimensions to the stories, and for bringing them to life again, and subsequently to print. To them I express appreciation and graditude. Simón Almendares R. translated some of the stories into Spanish and taught them to my college Spanish classes to the delight of the students, proving, to my satisfaction, that children's stories are effective with young-at-heart teachers and students. Anita Charney of Collier Macmillan International encouraged the publication of the stories and Linda Conoval is responsible for the format of the book. Both took a special interest in the project and seemed to place their hearts into the book. I owe, most of all, special appreciation to the editor, Peggy Intrator, who worked patiently with me on the stories, making useful and constructive suggestions. Peggy grew to love the stories and I know that from her feelings about them she grew to understand in Forestville California that animals really talk.

Forestville Tales

Renard the Fox and the Truck Full of Fish

(FRENCH)

Learn these words and expressions with your teacher.

fur   **play dead**
shiny   **is worried**

It's winter. Renard the Fox is very hungry but he is not worried. He is a very smart fox. He knows that he can find food for his family without a lot of work. He has a plan. On the road in the forest he sees two men driving a small truck. In the back of the truck there are two boxes full of fish. Renard decides to get some of those fish for himself and his family. First, he runs and gets far ahead of the truck. Then, he lies down in the road and plays dead. The truck moves slowly down the road. Soon the men in the truck see Renard the Fox.   1

"Look! There's a fox!" one man says to the other. "Let's stop and look at him." "He's dead. We can use his fur. Throw him into the truck!" the other man says. So the men throw Renard into the truck near the small box of fish. Then they go back 2 into the truck. While they are talking, Renard eats all the fish in the small box. When the truck slows down to turn, he 3 quickly takes the other box and jumps onto the road. "Hey there!" he calls to the men. "Thanks a lot for these delicious fish. I am going to keep my fur and these fish."

The men try to stop him, but Renard runs away. He is very 4 happy. Now he has fish for himself, his wife and their two children. They have enough to eat for the whole winter, and the fish keeps their fur looking nice and shiny.

Exercises

True/False

If the sentence is true, write "T." If the sentence is false, write "F."

Examples: _F_ It's summer.

_T_ Renard is hungry.

1. _____ Renard is a very stupid fox.

2. _____ He sees two men driving a bus.

3. _____ He sees two boxes of fish.

4. _____ The men want to use Renard's fur.

5. _____ The fish will keep the foxes' fur nice and shiny.

Vocabulary Practice

Choose one of the following words and write it in the correct space.

try	driving
throw	ahead
fish	keep

Example: Renard decides to get some of those _fish_ for himself and his family.

1. On the road in the forest Renard sees two men _____ a small truck.

2. He runs and gets _____ of the truck,

3. "_____ him into the truck!" the man said.

4. "I'm going to _____ my fur and these fish." Renard said.

5. The men _____ to stop him, but Renard runs away.

Fill Ins

Fill in the blanks with a word. It does not have to be the same word as in the story, but the sentence has to be correct. Try not to look back at the story until you are finished.

Renard the fox is _____ hungry, but he is not

_____ . He knows that he _____ find food for his

_____ without a lot of _____ . On the road in

_____ forest he sees two _____ driving a small

truck. _____ truck has two boxes _____ fish in

the back. _____ decides to get some _____ those

fish.

Write Your Own Sentences

1. Write three things that Renard does.

    Example: Renard runs ahead of the truck.

    a. _____ .

    b. _____ .

    c. _____ .

2. Write three things that Renard is (or is not).

    Example: Renard is not worried.

    a. _____ .

    b. _____ .

    c. _____ .

17

Silly Saburo

(JAPANESE)

Learn these words and expressions with your teacher.

coin	dig
firewood	dig up
pick up	tool box
chop up	is angry with someone

1

Saburo lives on a farm in Japan. Everybody calls him Silly Saburo. Saburo can't understand why, but maybe you can. For example, one day Saburo's father told him to go to the garden and dig up some potatoes. He told Saburo to put them in the sun to dry. Saburo went to the garden. While he was digging for potatoes he found an old box full of gold. Someone left it there a long time ago. Saburo didn't know what to do 1 with the gold. He remembered what his father said about the

2

3

potatoes, and decided to put the gold coins and the potatoes in the sun to dry. When he got home he told his father about the gold. His father ran to the garden, but it was too late. The gold was gone. 2

Of course, his father was angry. He told Saburo to put everything he finds in a bag and bring it home. The next day Silly Saburo was working in the garden again. He found a dead cat. He remembered what his father said and he put the dead cat in a bag. When he brought it home, his father was 3 angry and told him that he was very silly. He said, "When you find something like this dead cat, you should throw it into the river."

4

5

The next day Saburo found some firewood. He picked it up and threw it into the river. A neighbor was passing. She saw what Saburo did and told him not to throw away good wood. It was very good wood for a fire. She said, "When you find something like that, you should chop it up and take it home." 4

Well, on his way home, Saburo found his father's new tool box. The box was made of wood. He took an ax, chopped it up and brought it home. 5

Of course, his mother and father were very angry. "You stay at home and clean the house," his mother said, "I'll go out and do your work!"

Poor Silly Saburo. He doesn't understand why his parents are always so angry with him.

Exercises

True/False

If the sentence is true, write "T." If the sentence is false, write "F."

Examples: __F__ Saburo found a dead dog.

__T__ Saburo chopped up his father's tool box.

1. __F__ Saburo is very smart.

2. __T__ Saburo found a box of gold when he was digging in the garden.

3. __T__ Saburo put the gold in the sun to dry.

4. __F__ Saburo brought the firewood home.

5. __F__ Saburo understands why his parents are always angry with him.

Circle Exercise

Circle the correct word. Try not to look back at the story.

Saburo lives (in/**on**) a farm in Japan. One day, when he was digging (**in**/over) the garden he found some gold.

The (last/**next**) day he found a dead cat. When he brought (**it**/the) home, his (neighbor/**father**) was angry.

The next day Saburo found (a turtle/**some firewood**). Poor Silly Saburo. His mother wants him to stay (in/**at**) home and clean the house.

Vocabulary Practice

Choose one of the following words or phrases to finish each sentence.

took   ~~to dig up~~
a long time ago   threw
made of   ~~chopped up~~

Example: He took an ax and **chopped up** the tool box.

1. Saburo went to the garden _to dig up_ some potatoes.

2. Someone left a box of gold there _a long time ago._

3. He _took_ the dead cat home.

4. Saburo _threw_ the firewood into the river.

5. His father's tool box was _made of_ wood.

Fill Ins

Fill in the blanks with a word. It does not have to be the same word as in the story, but the sentence has to be correct. Try not to look back at the story until you are finished.

One day Saburo's father _told_ him to go to _the_ garden and dig up some _potatos_ . Saburo went to the _garden_ . When he was digging _he_ found a box full _of_ gold. He put the _gold_ coins in the sun _to_ dry.

The next day when _Saburo_ was working in the _garden_ ,he found a dead _cat_ . He brought it home. _Poor_ Silly Saburo. He doesn't _know_ why his parents are _always_ so angry with him.

The King of the Frogs

(AFRICAN)

Learn these words and expressions with your teacher.

is afraid	lazy
angry	loud
get angry	noise
brave	real
complain	splash
fight	threw
go back	touch
turn into	

A long time ago frogs used to make a lot of noise. They made much more noise than they make now. In fact, they made too much noise.

In order to control the noise they decided that they needed a king. So they went to their god Mumi and said they wanted a king.   1

2

3

Mumi was a very lazy god. He didn't want to look for a king. So, after the frogs left he picked up a big stone and threw it into the lake.   2

It hit the water with a loud splash. The frogs thought that the stone was their king. They were very happy.

Nobody made any noise. Nobody went near the stone. There were no fights. The lake was very quiet.

Of course, the "king" didn't move. He never said a word. Soon the frogs got brave. They got braver and braver. They swam close to the "king." They swam closer and closer.

One day one of the frogs got so brave that she touched the stone. She looked at it for a long time. Then she said, "This isn't a king. This is just a stone."   3

4

5

6

The frogs got very angry. They got angrier and angrier. They got so angry that they went to their god Mumi again. They complained, "We asked for a king and you only gave us a stone." This made the god very angry. "Go back to your lake," he said, "and I'll send you a real king."   4

After they left, Mumi took another stone and threw it into the lake. This time when the stone hit the water, it turned into a crocodile!   5

The crocodile swam quietly around the lake. The frogs swam close to the crocodile. They swam closer and closer.

The crocodile opened its mouth. It opened its mouth wider and wider. Then all of a sudden, it shut its mouth. The frogs were afraid.   6

After that the frogs didn't make as much noise as they used to. They were afraid that if they made too much noise the crocodile would find them. Today frogs still make noise. But if you go too near a lake, the frogs become very quiet. They are afraid that you are a crocodile.

Exercises

True/False

If the sentence is true, write "T." If the sentence is false, write "F."

1. _____ The frogs wanted a policeman to control their noise.

2. _____ Mumi was a lazy god.

3. _____ The frogs thought the stone was their king.

4. _____ One of the frogs got very brave.

5. _____ Frogs still make noise.

Vocabulary Practice

Choose one of the following words or phrases to finish each sentence.

to make	threw
happy	near
decided	turned into

Example: Mumi *threw* the stone into the lake.

1. The frogs *decided* that they needed a king.

2. Nobody went *near* the king.

3. The frogs were very *happy* .

4. The stone *threw* a crocodile.

5. Now the frogs are afraid *to make* noise.

Sentence Combining

Each number has two sentences. You are going to combine the two sentences into one, shorter sentence. Here's how. In the second sentence, a few words are underlined. Put the underlined word or words in the correct place in the first sentence to make the combined sentence.

Example: Frogs used to make noise.
They made a lot of noise.
Frogs used to make a lot of noise .

1. The frogs went to their god Mumi.
He was a <u>lazy</u> god.

_____

2. The stone hit the water with a splash.
It was a <u>very loud</u> noise.

_____

3. Mumi said, "Go back to your lake and I'll send you a king."
He said he would send a <u>real</u> king.

_____

4. The crocodile swam around the lake.
He swam around the <u>big</u> lake.

_____

Fill Ins

Fill in the blanks with a word. It does not have to be the same word as in the story, but the sentence has to be correct. Try not to look back at the story until you are finished.

A long time ago frogs used to _____ a lot of noise. They decided they _____ a king to control the noise. Their _____ Mumi didn't want to look for a _____.

He picked up a stone and _____ it into the lake. Nobody _____ any noise.

One day one of the frogs got _____ . She touched the stone. She said, "This _____ a king."

The frogs got angry. They _____ to their god Mumi again. This time _____ threw a stone that turned into a _____ . Now the frogs are afraid to _____ too much noise.

How the Mayans Got Fire and Fooled Their Enemies

(MEXICAN)

Learn these words and expressions with your teacher.

baskets	fool	Mayan
blanket	friendly	steal
chief	gift	stick
enemy	Indian	go out
feather	light/lit	

1

Many, many years ago the Mayans lived near a big lake. On the other side of the lake there was a different group of Indians. The two groups were enemies. The other group of Indians had fire and the Mayans didn't.

1

2

3

4

5

The Mayan chief wanted to get fire for his people. He knew that fire was very important for cooking and keeping warm.

He sent two of his men to ask the people on the other side of the lake for some of their fire. The men got in a boat and crossed the lake.

Those people wouldn't listen to the chief's men. They told them to leave and threw stones at their boats.   2

"Maybe they will be friendlier if I send them some gifts," the chief thought. He picked two other men and sent them across the lake. This time, the men took many beautiful and important gifts with them. They carried baskets of corn, beautiful hats with feathers, and blankets.   3

When they reached the other side of the lake, the people there were still not friendly. Again they told them to leave and threw stones at their boats.   4

The chief didn't know what to do. He spoke with all of the important men of his village.

They decided to steal some fire. This is how they did it. The Mayans had many dogs. The chief asked his people to find the most intelligent dog in the village. At last they found the dog. The chief put a stick in the dog's mouth and sent him across the lake.   5

6

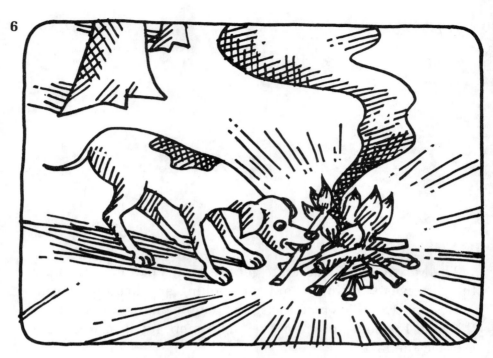

7

38

The dog swam to the other side of the lake. It was nighttime when he arrived and everybody was sleeping.

The dog walked quietly to the fire in the center of the village and lit the stick.   6

No one saw him as he walked back to the lake. He swam across the lake very slowly because he didn't want the fire to go out. He swam so slowly that it took all night to cross the lake.

In the morning he reached his village and walked carefully to the chief. The chief took the stick and started a fire in the center of the village. That is the way the Mayans fooled their enemies and got fire.   7

Exercises

True/False

If the sentence is true, write "T." If the sentence is false, write "F."

1. _____ A different group of Indians had fire.

2. _____ The other Indians gave the fire to the Mayans.

3. _____ The Mayan chief sent a dog to steal the fire.

4. _____ The dog swam quickly.

5. _____ The Mayans fooled their enemies.

Sentence Combining

Each number has two sentences. You are going to combine the two sentences into one, shorter sentence. Here's how. In the second sentence, a few words are underlined. Put the underlined word or words in the correct place in the first sentence.

Example: The Mayans lived near a lake.
It was a <u>very big</u> lake.

The Mayans lived near a very big lake.

1. There was a different group of Indians.
They lived <u>on the other side of the lake</u>.

A different group of Indians _lived on the other side_ _of the lake._

2. The Chief sent two men.
He sent them <u>across the lake</u>.

The chief sent two men across the b

3. The Chief spoke with the men of his village.
They were <u>important</u>.

The chief spoke with the important men _of his village._

4. The men picked a dog.
It was <u>very intelligent</u>.

The men picked a very intelligent _dog._

40

5. The dog swam across the lake.
He swam <u>slowly</u>.

The dog swam slowly. across the lake.

Verb Practice

Change the underlined verbs from the past to the present.
Example: The Mayans <u>lived</u> near a big lake.

The Mayans live near a big lake .

1. On the other side of the lake there <s>was</s> a different group of
Indians. _is_

_____ .

2. The other group <u>had</u> fire. _has_

_____ .

3. The Chief's men <u>carried</u> baskets of corn.

_____ .

4. He <u>swam</u> across the lake.

_____ .

5. He <u>didn't</u> want the fire to go out. _doesn't_

_____ .

Fill Ins

Fill in the blanks with a word. It does not have to be the same word
as in the story, but the sentence has to be correct. Try not to look
back at the story until you are finished.

Many years ago the Mayans didn't _have_ fire. On the
other side of _the_ lake where they lived there was a
different group of Indians. The other group _had_
fire, but the two groups were _enemies_ . The Mayan chief
wanted to get _some_ fire. He sent two of his _chiefs_
to ask the people on the _other_ side of the lake for some
_of_ their fire. Those people wouldn't listen.
the chief thought, "Maybe they will be _nicer_ if
I send them some _gifts_ ." The men took gifts, but the
other _Indians_ were still not friendly.

There's Always Room for More

(LATVIAN)

Learn these words and expressions with your teacher.

beggar	lie
box	pail
that was enough	room
I'm full	sand
full of	soup
hungry	stones
invite	

1

One day a hungry beggar went to the house of a rich man. He asked for something to eat. The rich man invited the beggar in and gave him some soup. The beggar drank the soup very quickly. When he finished the rich man asked, "Do you want more to eat?" "No, thanks," the beggar answered. "That was enough. I'm full."

But the rich man gave the beggar a large plate of meat. The beggar finished that very quickly also. "Do you want more to eat?" the rich man asked again. "No, thanks," the beggar answered. "That was enough. I'm full."

But the rich man didn't stop. He gave the beggar some delicious chocolate cake. The beggar quickly finished the food again.

1

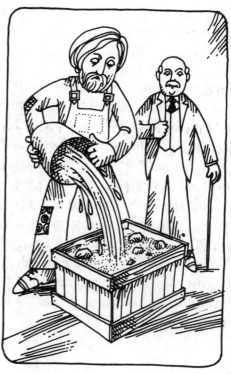

"Why do you lie to me?" the rich man asked. "Every time I ask you if you want more to eat, you say no; but every time I give you more, you eat it quickly."

2

The beggar looked around. Outside the kitchen there was a box. He filled the box with stones and asked the rich man, "Is this box full?" "Of course it's full," the rich man answered.

Then the beggar put some sand in the box that was full of stones. "Is this box full?" he asked again.

"Of course it's full," the rich man answered.

Then the beggar got a pail of water. He poured the water into the box that was full of stones and sand.

3

"You see," he said to the rich man. "Every time I ask you if the box is full, you say yes; but every time you say yes, I fill the box again. It's the same thing with the food you gave me. There's always room for more."

Exercises

True/False

If the sentence is true, write "T." If the sentence is false, write "F."

1. _T_ The beggar drank the soup and said that he was full.

2. _F_ The rich man gave the beggar some gold.

3. _T_ The beggar found a box in the kitchen.

4. _F_ The rich man said the box was beautiful.

5. _T_ The beggar filled the box many times.

Sentence Combining

Each number has two sentences. You are going to combine the two sentences into one, shorter sentence. Here's how. In the second sentence, a few words are underlined. Put the underlined word or words in the correct place in the first sentence to make the combined sentence.

1. The beggar went to a man's house.
   The man was <u>rich</u>.
   The beggar went to a rich man's house.

2. The man gave the beggar a plate of meat.
   The plate was <u>large</u>.
   The man gave the beggar a large plate of meat.

3. The man gave the beggar some cake.
   It was a <u>chocolate</u> cake.
   The man gave the beggar some chocolate cake.

4. The beggar finished the cake.
   It was <u>delicious</u>.
   The beggar finished the delicious cake.

5. The beggar put some sand in the box.
   The box was <u>full</u>.
   The beggar put some sand in the full box.

Fill Ins

Fill in the blanks with a word. It does not have to be the same word as in the story, but the sentence has to be correct. Try not to look back at the story until you are finished.

The beggar ate everything. The rich man _asked_, "Why do you lie to me?" The _beggar_ filled a box with stones and asked _the_ rich man, "Is this box full?" "Of _course_ it's full," the rich man said.

Then _the_ beggar put some sand in the box _that_ was full of stones. The rich man _said_ again that it was full. Then the beggar _put_ a pail of water. He _poured_ the water into the box full of stones and _sand_. There's always room for more!

Write Your Own Sentences

1. Write three things that the beggar did.
   a. _The beggar ate meat_.
   b. _The beggar asked can i eat some food_.
   c. _The beggar is full_.

2. Write three things that the rich man did.
   a. _The rich man gave some meat_.
   b. _The rich man gave some soup_.
   c. _Rich man asked the beggar wanted some food_.

Why the Rabbit Has a Short Tail and Long Ears

AFRICAN AMERICAN (SOUTHERN U.S.)

Learn these words and expressions with your teacher.

break off	**hurt**
Brother	**lucky**
fly/flew	**ouch!**
frozen	**shake/shook**
go fishing	**voice**
grab	**made someone angry**

1

A long time ago the rabbit had a long tail with lots of hair and short ears. Every time Brother Rabbit saw Brother Fox he shook his tail in the fox's face. This made Brother Fox very angry. He didn't want Brother Rabbit to shake his tail in his face. He tried thinking of a way to make him stop.

1

One day Brother Fox went fishing. He was lucky and went home with lots of fish. On the way home he saw Brother Rabbit. "How did you catch all of those fish?" Brother Rabbit asked. Brother Fox thought to himself, "Now I can teach the rabbit to stop shaking his tail in my face." Then he said to Brother Rabbit, "When the night is very cold, go down to the river and put your tail in the water. Let it stay there all night. In the morning, you'll have lots of fish. But don't tell anyone what you're doing because it's my secret way to catch fish." "Good," Brother Rabbit said. "I'll go fishing tonight." 2

3

4

5

The rabbit went down to the river. He put his tail in the water. It was very cold. He wanted to go home but he also wanted to catch lots of fish, so he stayed there all night. In the morning, the rabbit tried pulling his tail out of the water. It didn't come out. It was frozen in the water. He pulled and pulled but his tail didn't come out. Brother Rabbit was afraid that a man would come so he started screaming for help. "Help! Help! Help!" he called. 3

Brother Crow heard Brother Rabbit. "Where is Brother Rabbit?" he thought. "He needs help." So Brother Crow followed the rabbit's voice until he saw Brother Rabbit, sitting on the frozen water. He flew to help him. Brother Rabbit explained his problem. "I have an idea," the crow said. He grabbed the rabbit's right ear and started pulling. He pulled and pulled and the ear grew longer and longer. "Ouch!" the rabbit said. "You're hurting my ear. Try pulling my left ear." So the crow grabbed his left ear. He pulled and pulled and the rabbit's left ear grew longer and longer. 4

"Stop!" the rabbit screamed. He looked at himself in the water. "Do you see what you did? My ears are so long that now my best friends won't know me. Try pulling my tail." So Brother Crow grabbed Brother Rabbit's tail and started pulling. He pulled and pulled until the rabbit's tail broke off. 5

Since that day, rabbits have long ears and short tails and don't eat fish!

Exercises

True/False

If the sentence is true, write "T." If the sentence is false, write "F."

1. _F_ Brother Rabbit never shook his tail in Brother Fox's face.
2. _T_ Brother Fox wanted to teach Brother Rabbit to stop shaking his tail in his face.
3. _F_ It was a very warm night.
4. _T_ Brother Rabbit's tail was frozen in the water.
5. _F_ Brother Crow started pulling Brother Rabbit's nose.
6. _F_ Brother Rabbit's tail grew longer.

Verb Practice

Change the following sentences from the present tense to the past tense:

Example: Brother Rabbit shakes his tail in Brother Fox's face.
Brother Rabbit shook his tail in Brother Fox's face .

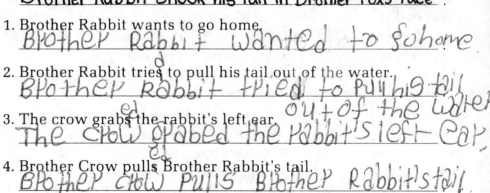

1. Brother Rabbit wants to go home.
   Brother Rabbit wanted to go home

2. Brother Rabbit tries to pull his tail out of the water.
   Brother Rabbit tried to pull his tail out of the water

3. The crow grabs the rabbit's left ear.
   The crow grabed the rabbit's left ear

4. Brother Crow pulls Brother Rabbit's tail.
   Brother Crow pulls Brother Rabbit's tail

Circle Exercise

Circle the correct word. Try not to look back at the story.

Brother Fox was lucky when (he/they) went fishing. He went home (with/for) lots of fish. Brother Fox wanted to teach Brother Rabbit to stop shaking his tail (to/in) his face. He told Brother Rabbit to keep his tail (at/in) the river all night.

The next morning, Brother Rabbit's tail was frozen (on/in) the water and he started screaming (for/with) help. Brother Crow flew (for/to) help Brother Rabbit.

Fill Ins fox made tail he fish

Fill in the blanks with a word. It does not have to be the same word as in the story, but the sentence has to be correct. Try not to look back at the story until you are finished.

Brother Rabbit always shook his _____ in Brother Fox's face. This _____ the fox angry. One day the _____ went fishing and was lucky. _____ went home with lots of _____.

The rabbit went down ___to___ the river and put his _____ in the water. It was ___very___ cold but he stayed there ___all___ night. In the morning he ___tried___ pulling his tail out of ___frozen___ water. It didn't come out. ___It___ was frozen in the water.

Jabuty, The Strongest Animal in the Forest

(BRAZILIAN)

Learn these words and expressions with your teacher.

rope	shell
shark	Wow!

One day Jabuty, a small brown turtle, went for a walk by the ocean.

While he was walking, a shark lifted his head out of the water, and said: "Hello, Mr. Short Legs. You have a very big shell. How can you walk with that big shell on those short legs?" This made Jabuty the turtle very angry. "Listen, Mr. 1 Shark," he said. "I have very short legs and my shell is big and heavy; but where I live, all my friends call me The Strong One. I'm stronger than you are!" When the shark heard this he laughed and laughed. "Show me how strong you are," he said.

"All right," Jabuty said. "I'm going to find a strong rope. I'm going to tie it around your tail and I'm going to pull you out of the water!" The shark laughed and laughed.

The turtle ran into the forest to find a strong rope.

While he was in the forest, he met a strong wild pig. "What are you looking for, Mr. Short Legs?" the pig asked Jabuty.

"I'm looking for a long rope."

"What are you going to do with it, Mr. Short Legs?"

"I'm going to show you how strong I am. I'm going to tie the rope around your neck and pull you down to the ocean."

The wild pig laughed and laughed. "That's a good game," she said.

Jabuty found a long rope and tied it around the pig's neck. He told the pig to count to fifty and then pull. 2

Then the turtle went down to the ocean. "Here I am," he said to the shark. "Now I'll tie this rope around your tail and run back into the forest. Count to twenty-five and swim away." "When I pull you into the water I'm going to eat you," the shark laughed.

Jabuty ran into the forest. He sat down and watched.

Soon the shark pulled. He pulled the pig towards the water.

"Wow! This turtle is really strong. I'll have to work harder," the pig said. Then she pulled. She pulled the shark towards the land.

"Wow! This turtle is really strong," the shark said. "I'll have to work harder."

The pig and the shark pulled and pulled while the turtle laughed and laughed. 3

Soon the shark and the pig got very tired and they rested. The turtle cut the rope.

He put the end of the rope into his mouth and went to the shark. "Now you know how strong I am," he told the shark. "Oh, yes," the shark said. "I'll never call you Mr. Short Legs again!" 4

Then Jabuty put the other end of the rope into his mouth and went to the pig. "Now you see how strong I am," he said to her. "Oh, yes," the wild pig said. "I'll never call you Mr. Short Legs again!" 5

Jabuty has many adventures. Read the next story and learn more about Jabuty.

Exercises

True/False

If the sentence is true, write "T." If the sentence is false, write "F."

1. _T_ Jabuty went for a walk by the ocean.

2. _F_ He talked with a pig who was swimming in the ocean.

3. _T_ The shark called Jabuty "Mr. Short Legs."

4. _F_ Jabuty talked with a shark who was walking in the forest.

5. _T_ The shark and the pig pulled and pulled and then thought Jabuty was very strong.

Verb Practice

Change the underlined verbs from past to future. (*Remember:* There are two ways to change a verb to the future tense.)

Example: Jabuty went for a walk by the ocean.

Jabuty will go for a walk by the ocean.
Jabuty is going to go for a walk by the ocean.

1. A shark lifted his head out of the water.

A shark will lifted his head soon.
soon.

2. The shark said something that made Jabuty angry.

Will said something,

3. The wild pig laughed.

The wild pig will laughed. tomorrow.
tomorrow.

4. Jabuty found a long rope yesterday.

Will found tomorrow rope, tonight.
tonight.

60

Circle Exercise

Circle the correct word or phrase. Try not to look back at the story.

Jabuty ran (where/into) the forest. He sat (up/down) and watched. The pig and the shark pulled and pulled (on/in) the rope. They got tired and rested. Jabuty cut the rope and put one end (of/from) it (into/on) his mouth. He went (with/to) the shark. Then Jabuty got the (another/other) end of the rope and went to the pig. The pig and the shark think that Jabuty (is/isn't) very strong.

Sentence Combining

Each number has two sentences. You are going to combine the two sentences into one, shorter sentence. Here's how. In the second sentence, a few words are underlined. Put the underlined word or words in the correct place in the first sentence to make the combined sentence.

1. Jabuty went for a walk.
   He walked <u>by the ocean</u>.
   Jabuty went for a walk by the ocean

2. Mr. Shark lifted his head.
   It came <u>out of the water</u>.
   Mr. Shark lifted his head out of the water

3. "I'm going to pull you," Jabuty said.
   "You'll come <u>out of the water</u>."
   "I'm going to pull you out of the water," Jabuty said.

4. Jabuty met a pig in the forest.
   The pig was <u>strong</u>.
   Jabuty met a strong pig in the forest.

5. The pig and the shark pulled the rope.
   They were strong and pulled <u>very hard</u>.
   The pig and the shark pulled the rope very hard.

Jabuty, The Turtle and Fury, The Jaguar

(BRAZILIAN)

Learn these words and phrases with your teacher.

come out
fall asleep
pretend

talk about
fool someone

1

Do you remember how smart Jabuty was when he made the shark and the wild pig think that he was the strongest animal in the forest? Soon all the animals in the forest were talking about Jabuty. When Fury the Jaguar heard the story he became very angry. After all, jaguars are big, strong animals. They are also very fast. So one day Fury went to look for Jabuty. He found him by the river where most turtles go because they like to swim. "Jabuty," he said, "the other animals say that you are the strongest one in the woods. They say you are stronger than the shark and stronger than the wild pig. Well, I don't believe it. I'm King of the forest. I like to eat fresh meat and I'm going to eat you."

1

When Jabuty heard what Fury the Jaguar said, he was very frightened. But Jabuty was very smart; so after thinking for a few seconds, he said, "I know you are the King and that you like to eat fresh meat, but I think that I can eat more meat than you."

"I don't believe you," Fury said. "Let's see how much meat you can eat." Fury got two very big pieces of meat. He gave one of the pieces to Jabuty and said, "Now we'll see who can eat the most."

"Okay," Jabuty said, "but promise to close your eyes when you eat because I can't eat with my eyes open."

Fury laughed and said, "That's okay." They started to eat. Fury ate very fast. He ate faster than Jabuty. He ate so much **2** and so fast that he got very tired, and because his eyes were closed he fell asleep.

As soon as Fury fell asleep, Jabuty changed his piece of meat with the little piece of meat that Fury left. Then he shouted to the jaguar, "Hey, Fury, I can't eat any more. Open your eyes and you'll see who ate the most."

The jaguar opened his eyes. He saw that he had a big piece of meat in front of him but Jabuty had only a small piece of meat. "It's true," he said to Jabuty. "You can eat more meat than I can. But I am the fastest animal in the forest. Tomorrow we'll have a race to the river. Then we'll see who can run the fastest." **3**

"Alright," the turtle said, "I'll meet you tomorrow by the tall rubber tree when the sun comes up." Jabuty went home and told his family about the race. They talked and talked the whole night. In the morning they had a plan to fool the jaguar.

4

5

6

The next day Jabuty went to the tall rubber tree. He got there when the sun came up. Fury arrived at the same time. "Now let's see who can run the fastest," Jabuty said to Fury. Fury laughed and laughed.

"Ha, ha, ha," he laughed. "I can run faster than you. I'm the fastest animal in the forest." 4

"Let's start." Jabuty said. Fury started to run. He ran as fast as he could. After a few minutes he stopped and looked back. He couldn't see the turtle anywhere. But while he was looking back, one of Jabuty's brothers came out from behind a small tree. He was far ahead of Fury. The jaguar started to run. He 5 saw Jabuty's brother and ran past him. He was very surprised, but he kept on running. A few minutes later he stopped again to look back. While he was looking back another one of Jabuty's brothers came out from behind another small tree. He was far ahead of the jaguar. Fury started to run again. He 6 saw Jabuty's other brother and ran past him. He was very

surprised again, but he kept on running. A few minutes later he stopped again to look back. The same thing happened again and again.

7

When Fury finally arrived at the river, Jabuty's oldest brother was waiting there. He pretended to be Jabuty. "You see," Jabuty's brother said to Fury, "I'm faster than you. I arrived at the river before you did."

"You're right," Fury said. "You're stronger than the shark, you're stronger than the wild pig, you can eat more than I can and you're faster than I am. You're the fastest and strongest animal in the forest. I won't try to eat you. I'll never bother you again."

8

And that's what happened. None of the animals in the forest bothers the turtle. And that's why the turtle doesn't have any enemies in the forest.

Exercises

True/False

If the sentence is true, write "T." If the sentence is false, write "F."

1. _____ Fury found Jabuty on top of a tree.

2. _____ The jaguar likes to eat fresh meat.

3. _____ Jabuty said he could eat more meat than the jaguar.

4. _____ The jaguar fell asleep because his eyes were closed.

5. _____ Jabuty and Fury decided to have a bicycle race.

6. _____ Jabuty's family helped him fool the jaguar.

Verb Practice

Choose one of the following words or phrases to finish each sentence.

became	ahead
shouted	race
fell	comes up
pretended	look back

1. The jaguar heard about Jabuty's story and _____ very angry.

2. The jaguar ate some meat and soon _____ asleep.

3. Jabuty _____ , "Open your eyes and see who ate the most."

4. Tomorrow we'll have a _____ to see who can run the fastest.

5. They decided to meet in the morning when the sun _____ .

6. Jabuty's brother was far _____ of Fury.

7. Fury stopped to _____ but he couldn't see the turtle anywhere.

8. The turtle's oldest brother _____ to be Jabuty.

70

Sentence Combining

Each number has two sentences. You are going to combine the two sentences into one, shorter sentence. Here's how. In the second sentence, a few words are underlined. Put the underlined word or words in the correct place in the first sentence to make the combined sentence.

1. Fury found Jabuty.
   The turtle was by the river.

   _____

2. The jaguar said, "Tomorrow we'll have a race."
   "We'll race to the river."

   _____

3. In the morning the turtles had a plan.
   They wanted to fool the jaguar.

   _____

4. The jaguar started to run.
   He ran as fast as he could.

   _____

5. The jaguar stopped and looked back.
   He did this after a few minutes.

   _____

Write Your Own Sentences

1. Write four things that Fury said to Jabuty.

   a. _____ .

   b. _____ .

   c. _____ .

   d. _____ .

2. Write four things that Jabuty said to Fury.

   a. _____ .

   b. _____ .

   c. _____ .

   d. _____ .